PROMESAS: GEOGRAPHY OF THE IMPOSSIBLE

GLORIA VANDO

Arte Público Press
Houston
Texas
1993

⎤ the National Endowment for the
⎤n and the Mellon Foundation.
⎤ slightly different form, in the

The Denny Poems, 1991–1992, Lincoln College, Lincoln, Illinois ("HE2-104: A True Planetary Nebula in the Making"—first place 1991, Billee Murray Denny Poetry Contest); *Environment: Essence & Issue*, Pig Iron Press ("Learning My Name," "Glimpses of Light"); *The First Anthology of Missouri Women Writers*, Sheba Review, Inc. ("Out of Bounds in Kansas"); *Helicon Nine*, Helicon Nine, Inc. ("Return to the City of Holy Faith"); *Kansas City Out Loud II*, BkMk Press, University of Missouri ("Field Day," honorable mention, Billee Murray Denny Poetry Contest; "Moving Pictures"); *Kenyon Review* ("Fire"); *Looking for Home*, Milkweed Editions, ("Chimayó"); *New Letters* ("Los Alamos," "Promesas"); Poets On ("My Father, on the Other Hand"); *Seattle Review* ("Faith"); *Stiletto One* ("Cante Jondo," "Commonwealth, Common Poverty," "Divorce," "In the Dark Backward," "Knife," "Latchkey Kid," "My Mother Cunning Yet Innocent," "New York City Mira Mira Blues," "Psychomachia").

I am grateful to the Kansas Arts Commission for a Poetry Fellowship on which these poems were written, and to the Money for Women / Barbara Deming Memorial Fund, Inc., for financial help and moral support.

I thank E. S. Miller, David Ray, Ann Slegman, and Donna Trussell for their suggestions, encouragement, and thoughtful attention to the poems, and Anita Velez-Mitchell, my mother, for all of the above, and for passing on to me her love of the language and the culture and the people of Puerto Rico.

Arte Público Press
University of Houston
Houston, Texas 77204-2090

Cover design by Mark Piñón
Original painting by María Antonia Ordóñez
"A caballo de mentiras," Copyright ©1985
Author photograph by David Remley

Vando, Gloria
    Promesas: Geography of the Impossible / Gloria Vando.
        p.   cm.
    ISBN 1-55885-061-9: $16.95 — ISBN 1-55885-059-7 (pbk.): $8.00
    1. Puerto Ricans—New York (N.Y.)—Poetry. I. Title.
PS3572.A67P76 1992   92-28053
    811'.54–dc20   CIP

The paper used in this publication meets the requirements of the American National Standard for Permanence of Paper for Printed Library Materials Z39.48-1984. ∞

To Bill
and
to Lorca, Paul, and Anika
promises kept

Forth I fared, and now in vain
Seek to find the place again . . .
List, and learn from what is passed,
Having bliss, to hold it fast.
—"The Fountain of Youth,"
from *The Land of Cockaigne*, 13th century

Your Highnesses have an Other World here, by
which our holy faith can be so greatly advanced
and from which such great wealth can be drawn.
—Christopher Columbus
in a letter to the Sovereigns
on the Third Voyage, October 18, 1498

The Lands of Cockaigne were utopias . . . all
locate[d] in a distant somewhere else, in a lost isle
at the heart of an ocean . . . The same geography
of the impossible explains why certain Europeans
believed in the "American Mirage." Newly discov-
ered by the great Renaissance voyages, the people
of America were assigned virtues that Europe had
long since lost. Moreover, upon contact with civ-
ilization, these native American virtues vanished
away.
—Jean Delumeau, *Sin and Fear*, 1983

Oh, poor Puerto Rico, Puerto Pobre
—Pablo Neruda

CONTENTS

III. Singing the Land

Promesas:
Geography of the Impossible

I. In the Dark Backward

Prospero: ... What seest thou else
In the dark backward and abysm of time?

        · · ·

Miranda: O, the heavens!
What foul play had we, that we came from thence?
Or blessed was't, we did?
        Prospero: Both, both, my girl.

Fire

The fire broke out in 1B, the garden
apartment where the Irish family
lived—the rest of us, the Puerto Ricans,
relegated to inland brown rooms
that blotted out the memory of hope,
the cornflower blue of skies over
Luquillo, the crimson country roads
painted with petals from flamboyáns,
the fuchsia hands of oleander waving
for us to come back, come back,
come back to the healing seas
of Isla Nena, the beaches rich with gold.
It was an upstairs hell, this darkness,
this gloom, this view of brick
and cement and dried pigeon dung.

An ugly green stairwell gnawed its way
up through the center of this urban silo,
its bare bulbs flickering a neon stain
on the drained faces of tenants
stopping to rest on every landing,
to catch their breath, to lean
for a moment or two on the handrail,
wondering where exactly they had made
a wrong turn, a wrong choice, knowing
(despite rumors they were transient)
that there was no turning back,
that the only paths left to them led
to other stairwells in other tenements,
to other windows facing other brick walls.

When the fire broke out that morning
Abuelita was making the beds, a ritual
she enjoyed, and I enjoyed watching—
the perfect corner she could control,
the coverlet she could smooth with a slow
sweep of her hand, urging all creases
to disperse—a gesture I would remember today,
sitting at a ball park 50 years and 1500 miles away,

watching boys in royal blue chase
air pockets trapped beneath the stadium tarp
out into the chill night—an escape
Abuelita would never know but always long for.

Like indulgences during the Middle Ages,
rents in New York City are scaled
according to height—the nearer to God
the apartment, the higher the rent—
and nearest to God were we
on the 6th floor of that eastside tenement
when fire, like pride incensed, found voice
and screamed through the inarticulate darkness
of the dumbwaiter, cursing the heavens,
the forgotten covenant, the silence.

Sirens and bull horns ordered us to evacuate.
A neighbor's son banged on our front door,
yelling *¡Fuego! ¡Fuego!* before racing
down the steps ten at a time, the thump
of his sneakers growing fainter and fainter.

Abuelita sighed and stopped making the bed.
She instructed me to wash my face
and hands. Sitting at her vanity,
she studied the sorrow etched around
her mouth. She smiled, applied a circle
of rouge to each raised cheek and
a sliver of pomade to her lips. Then
she shut her eyes and patted her face
with a pink velvet puff. Particles
of powder spiraled in the lamplight
like flurries of snow. I was enthralled.
She brushed her hair back into a bun
and fastened it with long silver hairpins.
Finally she stood, looked at her tall,
ample figure in the full-length mirror
and shook her head. Moments later,
she emerged from the bedroom in
a different black print dress, a brooch
of silver and onyx pinned to its lapel.

She put on a black straw hat, lowered
the veil over her eyes, took her purse and
gloves in one hand, my still damp hand
in the other, and led me out the door.

We descended in slow-motion zigzags
toward daylight and life and
lies we would come to accept as truths.
By the time we reached the 3rd floor
landing, we were greeting neighbors
returning from a moment's safety
to a higher, more insidious level
of salvation. The fire was contained.
But my grandmother and I were ready—
as ready as we would ever be.

My Mother Cunning Yet Innocent

My mother cunning yet innocent,
grabbing the new moon by its promise
and whistling through the suave sky
for an easy escape to where stardom
should have been but seldom was.

My mother split like a seasoned log
ready for burning yet whole and immutable
as bronze, her slender arms unbendable,
her teeth clenched behind
an ardent Rita Hayworth smile.

Still ill-defined she slips away,
gathering herself up into the thinnest
sliver of equivocation, falling
between folds of supple logic until
she's almost out of earshot.
But I'm obsessed with the mystery,
shout after her *Wait! Wait!*

The air is heavy with gardenias and sweet
tobacco. Smoke rings from her lips
drift out of sight like elliptic vows
while I strain to capture them
on my tiny wrists and fingers
not knowing then, no, not yet knowing—

My Father, on the Other Hand

My father, on the other hand, did
no more than lend his name
and leave a photograph I tinted
matching his emerald tie to our eyes.

Early in my life he left, returning
late, so late I do not know
his long hair sleek, shimmering white
like a lake about to freeze.

Uninvited, he plunges past his image
into my icy thoughts hoping
to be in the nick of time, hoping
to shatter the mirrored surface

of my calm. Pools part within pools.
Shards sharpened by that forced
baptism rise menacingly from the deep.
Yet I remain curiously inviolate.

Moving Pictures

Sometimes I see in movie stills,
overexposed moments, where figures
in white linen cluster conspiratorially,
the creases in their clothes
captured like faults with genetic
repercussions. The streets and
houses in these stills are whitewashed,
the light oblique, deflected by
low-lying clouds that seem suspended
from the sky like baffles in
a concert hall. Hushed glimpses
of another time I cannot quite recall.
They intrude at queer moments when
I am unprepared—brushing my teeth,
let us say, or washing my face,
I may look up from the porcelain
to blank eyes or someone else's smile
clenched behind a steamy veil. Or
stooping to caress the graceful slope
of a columbine in a courtyard,
my hand sticks to the moment and for
one second before my fingers recoil,
a hand about to touch the curve
of someone's cheek skips decades,
insinuates itself into my joy. The light
is bright. Too bright. It fades
the features on that little upturned face,
the expectation in those eyes. Only
a close-up of the hand remains.
Hard. Seamed. Like a mannequin's.

Practitioner

It was my grandfather who fed me,
cut my meat into little cubes and
made me chew while he counted every bite

> *mastica tu comida, niña—*
> *uno, dos, tres, cuatro, cinco . . .*

Not my grandmother—it was she
who held me to her bosom, soothing
as valerian blooms, muting terrors
of labyrinthine chases in the night.
Somehow I had assumed she took care
of all the little things—eucalyptus baths,
sobitos with Bay Rum, shampoos—
then today, while at a friend's house,
the smell of soap, a green smell, burst
free from my thick foam gloves, brushing
past my cheek in a hurried kiss and

I suddenly feel my grandfather's hands
on mine, hands as soft as a woman's,
rubbing a bar of Palmolive soap
across my lifeline, massaging the suds
down each finger, under each nail,
scrubbing away all signs of danger,
all threats of disease, all *microbios*,
rinsing, rinsing until the water
is safe, then with a clean white cloth
absorbing every alien drop. I see him

standing over me, his white shirt-sleeves
rolled halfway up his forearms,
the gold watch fob like a jump rope
slack across his vest, his black
leather case of magic potions—
mercurochrome, tincture of myrrh,
castor oil, *iodine*—threatening me
from a corner of the foyer.
He studies my impeccable offering,

first one side, then the other, before
he allows me to join my grandmother
at the table, when the count to five
begins again

> *uno, dos, tres, cuatro, cinco* ...
> *mastica tu comida, niña—*

My grandmother soothed me, but it was
my grandfather who kept me alive.

Malcriada

Te voy a dar una paliza, muchacha,
my grandfather threatens, as
he pulls the strap from his beltloops
and in one fell swoop snaps it against
the seat of a chair with a resonating

fffwitt! Then holding his pants up
with his free hand, he waves
the strap in the air like a lasso and
gives the chair two more swift slaps—
fffwitt! fffwitt!—to satisfy
my grandmother in the other room

and silence my giggles. His cheeks
turn as red as a clown's, his blonde
curls tremble like cooked fusilli,
his eyes narrow down to two tiny
slits of sky—while I, convinced he
is putting on a show for me, fall

to the floor convulsed with laughter.
¡Muchacha! he pleads, unable
to keep a straight face. Then shaking
his head, he sighs—*¡Ay bendito!*—digs
into his vest pocket, and gives me
two new pennies for an Eskimo Pie.

Divorce

On Saturdays her grandmother
would strip her bed and open
the windows while her grandfather
rolled the mattress up against
the head of the yellow iron frame
and carried her piggyback from
room to room. On this Saturday
she sneaks back into her room
and hides in the core of the striped
sleeve, wadding her body
into a rigid ball, small enough
and tight enough so no one
can find her; tight, tighter
so she can withstand the weight
of the horsehair, resist the steel
buttons embossing her flesh,
the fresh fumes of urine. Only
her blood boasts in the silence.
It is safe. She cannot see them
coming, cannot hear their reasons
why they're sending her away,
or hear their cries as they search
each empty room, while she—
ensheathed in the one bed they
will leave behind—awaits
the onslaught, hoping they'll forgive
whatever she has done, hoping
they'll forget that she must go.

Confianzuda

she touched me
and my whole body
convulsed
revolted by the shock
of her palm
her bad taste
in holding my arm
with the same hand
the same hand
that stroked
my father's face
away from us
turning it
to a far off place
promising satin
and jasmine
pearl seas and
ruby lips
parted and waiting
hour after dumb hour
while we in twilight
mourned

Sailor Suit

She tells him how when she is hurt
she is six again, always six, waiting
in the vestibule of a hospital,
a nurse at her side, waiting
for her grandmother and her mother
to come and take her home.

She is wearing a blue pleated skirt,
white middy blouse, red jacket
with a gold anchor on the pocket,
and a white patch over her left eye—
the perfect little patriot.

It is 1942. Her first war.

She tells him how when she aches
it is always the same low fist
that slams up hard against
her heart and tears her breath away.

When her mothers come for her
they take her to a park. They
sit on a bench and feed the pigeons.
She wants to go home, pulls them
by the hand. They are like monuments
of stone. They do not move.

Her grandmother tells the sky
she is going away. Her mother
tells the trees she is going away.
They tell each other she is going away
to a school with many girls her age,
a school in the mountains

cloistered by hemlocks and pines,
life-sprung with peonies, snowballs,
and a victory garden yielding
carrots and rhubarb and corn.

And the fist comes
and brands its shape into her heart.

Whenever she is hurt, she tells him,
she is six again, in her sailor suit,
begging them on her knees to keep her,
promising to make them coffee
every morning, to make their beds,
clear the table, run errands—*anything*
to make them love her.

They tell their hands that she must go,
they tell their shoes that she must go;
they take her to a nearby church
and tell Jesus that she must go.
The incense stabs at her heart,
oozes from her palms, staining her
lifeline a deep blue. She tells him
prayers are for the hopeful.

He tells her she can throw away
her sailor suit *forever*.

Visiting Day at School

My mother is sitting on a swing.
She wears a dark hat with a striped
feather standing at attention.

The jacket of her grey suit
is buttoned at the waist. Lace
cascades in gentle waves from her neck.

Her long legs cross at the ankles,
the toes of her pumps in the sand anchor
her swaying body. Motherless children

surround her, touch her, vie to push her
on the swing. She smiles the open smile
of stars. I am thinking, oh,

she is an angel come to take me home.
I want to go to her, claim her,
but there is no room for me, no room.

Prayer

Padre Nuestro
began the prayer
Abuelita taught me
but my children never learned
praying instead to *Adonoi* in Hebrew
which my grandmother never dreamed existed
and I, at six, falling away from her
falling somewhere
in the nondescript middle
at Hunt's Point Presbyterian Church with
Our Father, though the words were foreign
and my father had disappeared
with a nineteen-year-old
not much younger than my mother
yet I am to pray to Him and him
to come to me, save me
though I'm not sure which him if any can hear
my solemn hymn on Sunday
when the other girls and I walk
from boarding school to church
wearing clothes too large
for our awkward spindly frames
unused to dressing up
cringing from the lace, the lies
because in fact we are not loved—
and I grow up singing praises to his name
who forgets not his own
yet does not remember
the tight circumference of my arms
or his face in mine
so that I too do not know who I am
or which he makes cameo appearances
now and then, in dreams
I can't recall at daybreak
Padre, Father, Papi
invisible as the angel my mother swears
is watching over me while I grow up
with Papi in my corazón, Father in my head
Padre Nuestro in my craw—the crucified one

hurt, folded, bleeding—making me
angry and confused and guilty
for resenting Him who suffered so for me
and no matter how hard I sing
Great is Thy faithfulness O God, my Father
or how loudly I call his name
I know he will not respond—he is gone
like magic, moving in a mysterious way
but moving away—because men leave
early you learn they leave
with or without mumbo jumbo
they leave, leave their women
in black, in *luto*, in crape
engulfed in darkness
the inner light eternal-
ly dimmed like
a wasted bulb
in the spirit's
socket
ah men.

Letters from My Sister

Mi querida hermanita, she'd begin
in letter after letter, writing
to me in her six-year-old script
from a convent in New Jersey where
she said they made her wear
her undergarments in the shower—
the body a vile thing, apt to melt
or turn to stone if touched or seen.

She would write and plead with me
to come to her; but I, too, had been
sentenced to a life of negation,
reeking with the musty scent of sin
at a Catholic school in Ossining—
a somersault away from Sing Sing prison—
where my stepfather, an Argentinian,
who courted ritual and rules
so he could forego the one and break
the others, hoped I'd be saved.

I was Protestant, ostracized
to a room in a wing far enough away
from the main dorm that my
asthmatic wheezes—my due penance
for straying from the true faith—
would go unheard. I entertained
myself by blowing out the light fuses
and jumping to freedom from
my second-story bedroom window.

Oh, I was a dark soul, they told me—
and all around me light and love
and eternal salvation.

The habits of the nuns billowed
in my ten-year-old imagination,
billowed into gowns out of
Gone With the Wind—layers
and layers of ecru flouncing

through hallways, on staircases,
in the nave, the confessional,
racing across the meadow—but
always with purpose, like cats
never making extraneous moves.

The nuns would march to Mass,
to class, rush to keep us from
annoying the grounds keeper
teasing one another, or tormenting
them each time we'd stand up on
the swing and pump it back and
forth, back and forth, higher
and higher and *higher*, until
it would loop over the bar, float
over the bars, and sail down
the Hudson like a magic raft, ready
to take us home, to take us *home*—

Mi querida hermanita,
Today I prayed that someday
we could all live together in
a big red house with flowers.

Sister Marie de Lourdes, robust
and sly with an undiscernible smile
and large watery eyes that seemed
just to have witnessed a crime,
was always first at the scene,
her tsk-tsk-tsk-tsk-tsk announcing
her proximity, her skirts setting
the air in motion around her
like a giant bell, releasing strange
dark mysteries. One evening
after lights out, I decided to see
if what Gregoria had said was true:

"That's the first thing they do,"
she swore on the Bible, "they shave
their heads." As soon as I got my eye
to the keyhole, the girls behind me began

to prod me for details.
I held my breath and held up
fingers while Sister disrobed:

one—the collar, *two*—the smock,
three—the tunic, *four*—the skirt,
five—the slip, *six*—the petticoat—
and still she was fully dressed—
but slim now, so slim and frail
I felt ashamed, as if I had uncovered
a terrible secret—a secret quite different
from the one I had hoped to learn.
A door creaked in the hallway and
we scattered like loose beads to our beds.

Mi querida hermanita,
Today Sister told me I cannot go
to heaven because of Papi's divorce.
What does that mean? Promise
you won't go without me—promise.

Did I ever answer her, I wonder?
Did I ever tell her that her letters
made me feel I had a direct line
to my father's heart? In the photos
all his children look like me—
the same nose, the same sad eyes,
the same big smiles.

Latchkey Kid

Instead of butterscotch caramels
glistening in a Baccarat jar
her house is dark
bitter chocolate, so dark
shadows cringe in the corners,
clouds surround it low and hoarse
like a bad head cold in December.
At night insistent drafts lick
the threshold, stretching their
rough tongues across the hearth.
Her bones ache, feel like popsicle
sticks stained lime, sucked dry.
She never wants to go home.
It smells of death.
She goes instead to a friend's
house after school, outstays
her welcome through Fritolays,
pork chops, awkward
conversation as parents' eyes
exchange impatience. She lies
she will be going in a while, but
she's afraid and cannot tell them
her house is dark,
dark like her mother's blood,
dark like the crimson rose her father
sent for her seventh birthday,
a rose with a smudged note
he did not write.
She keeps its tall, brittle stem
in a bottle beside her bed. When
she turns on the light
it casts a shadow across her life.

In the Dark Backward

for Nina

How is it I was not raised
on the riverfront block
with the tall trees and a tall woman
calling my name, the sweetness
of warm peaches on her breath,
her arms like soft vowels
cushioning me from death? Why
is it I was confined to night,
forced to travel the shaft tunnel
below Manhattan before alighting
blonde and blue-eyed in Washington
Heights, where your mother
would add another plate for supper
and, long after the sun
had painted the Palisades across
the Hudson a deep bronze, wonder
aloud whether I'd be going soon?
I would pretend I had not heard
so I could stay until the moon
rose over the cliffs, when we'd
slip out and walk across the bridge
to the Jersey side where we'd sit
on the rocks and talk and watch
the early morning light patch up
the city's wounds. Was it Godly spite
that bore me to the wrong block
far from your haven on Haven Avenue—
or was it luck that locked
me in that dry-dock, where nothing but
my mind could billow in the breeze
and only the cries of kindred
children, like windswept echoes from
a ghost ship, could free my grief?

Coping Skills

I said how sad it was
     to have had no father.
She said how bad it was
     to have had an uncle
who fondled you
     under the covers.
I said he was a criminal.
She said he was a good man,
     a product of his culture.
I said if he could think
for himself he should
     have known better.
Better than he, she said,
     there were few.
I said she must be kidding.
She said, scout's honor—
     he was a saint.
But the fondling? I asked.
Oh, she said, he meant
     nothing by it,
it was his way of telling me
     he loved me.
She remembers everything.
I remember nothing.

My Life as a Book of Fiction

All family stories are myths about yourself.
—Russell Banks

With my aunt will die the secrets
of my childhood, secrets no one
can corroborate—I least of all,

for I remember nothing, except
the cocoa butter of her hands
on mine, my heart swelling with love

at this slight gesture—all else is gone
to that place where nightmares flourish.
My aunt is growing old. I try

to keep my life alive till I
can worm it back from her safekeeping,
back before she slips, revises

scenes or splices them with slices
of some other life. I find her
children's history intruding on

my own, a date fudged here, a season
there. Sometimes a year bobs up and
down in the ebbing waves of her

remembering. I try to catch each
day, bring it to the right conclusion
with a minimum of editing

but we're already on the fourth
or fifth edition. I see the
the galleys of my life unfold, fraught

with errors, omissions, dangerous
legends and, before long, addenda—
left to *me*, a total stranger.

—for Betty

II. On This Bitch of an Earth

Anoche soñé que oía
a Dios, gritándome: ¡Alerta!
Luego era Dios quien dormía,
y yo gritaba: ¡Despierta!
　　　　　　—Antonio Machado

That's how it is on this bitch of an earth.
　　　　　　—Samuel Beckett

Soy poeta por la estética
pero político por la ética.
　　　　　　—Pablo Neruda

Legend of the Flamboyán

1.

It was a good old-fashioned
victory—no massacres, no fires,
no children gunned down
in the streets of day,
no cameras to point a finger
and say *he* did it, or *they*;
it was calm, it was civilized—
they emerged from the ocean,
and claimed their paradise.

From the rain forest, naked and
trembling beneath scheffleras
and figs, perched like purple
gallinules among the low branches
of the jacarandas, the Taínos
watched the iron-clad strangers
wade awkwardly ashore, their
banners staking out their land.

Chief Agüeybana also watched,
the gold *guanín* glinting
on his chest like a target.
Who were these intruders and what
were they doing on this island?
Could they be cannibals like
the Caribes? Could they be gods?
Their bodies glistened like stars;
their eyes like the sea.

The Taínos met and argued
well into the night, weighing
the pros and cons of strategies—
if these were gods, to ignore them
might incite their wrath,
to fight them might invite death.
Best to rejoice then and welcome
the silver giants to Boriquén.

The Spaniards responded by
taking first their freedom,
then their land, then
using them as human picks to dig
for gold—gold for the crown,
gold for the holy faith,
gold for the glory of Spain.

2.

The darkness of the mines
consumed them, sapped
their laughter, their song,
locking them into perpetual night.
The women withdrew, drew in,
their hearts hard
against the longing they saw
in the strangers' eyes—
not to look, not to be seen—
they bowed their heads, folded
into themselves like secrets
whispered only in the safety
of brown arms.

3.

A wrecked vessel washed ashore
at Guajataca. The children raced
down to the beach looking
for treasures, looking under
torn sails, beneath coiled ropes,
turning over loosened boards,
and suddenly—a hand, then a face,
the skin pale and mottled, the eyes
staring up at them, opaque
like a fish, the color of the sea.

Something dead. Something *ungodly*.

The island echoed their cries.

That night the Taínos planned
carefully, knowing—
like those at Masada before them—
that there was no other way.
They drew straws.

The first Spaniard to awaken
was startled by the hush, as though
the earth itself had given up.
He stepped out into the chill,
into the stained silence,
but saw only flowers, thousands
of flamboyáns—

splashes of blood—

blooming all over the island.

Cry Uncle

for Carlos Velez-Rieckehoff

They say he was a revolutionary
in single-handed combat with contemporary
conquistadors who invaded his island's shores.
They say he was a radical, hitting hard,
baffling the foe, then running for cover
to the hills in and around Ciales, Novillo,
and points west where Yankee soldiers,
lost in the intricacies of hollows,
underbrush, and overload, deigned to follow.

They say, they say—but what they say is buried
like cloves of garlic deep into the diagonal slits
of my uncle's blue-grey eyes, and what I see
across from me is a mild, bearded old man who sits
eating quiche at Columbus Restaurant, haunt
of the undaunted: Madonna, Penn, Baryshnikov—
a far cry from revolution, *patria, libertad.*

My uncle's pale suit matches his eyes.
My mother, her hands on her brother's,
tries to woo him with a clone smile.
In vain. He sees her coquetry as puerile
next to the manly courage his island demands.
(In the photo my husband later will take,
my mother will lean toward her brother, he
toward me, and I, stalwart as a tree,
try to keep the house of Medina from toppling down—
yes, I, the youngest, am doomed to pillarhood.)

Besides my uncle's suit and his eyes
and the veins straddling tendons
across the backs of his laced hands, another
blueness infiltrates his person, hones his mirth.
It bruises the edge of every gesture,
every word, pares slogans down to sighs.

He turns to me now. But I am dry,

rebellion sucked from my bones early on.
There's no one left to justify
his failure, to render his lifelong mission holy.

The "cry" in the title also refers to The Cry of Lares (*El Grito de Lares*), a symbol of Puerto Rico's ongoing struggle for independence.

Cante Jondo

Segovia says Lorca was killed
by a jealous lover, but I know
that isn't so. I know he was seized
from midnight reverie, pried screaming
from the poem in his head, the lover
beside him pleading with Franco's men
before the butt end of a German carbine
careened him into a wordless sleep
taking him worlds away from Lorca,
Guernica, and the caves of Andalucía,
from the fifth column, the Falange, death—
far, far from death, deep into a dream
sweetened by seas, seeping slowly
into Moroccan fields where boys
culipandeando ignite the lighteyed
lust of tourists who come down
to excavate their scraggy yield—
Arabs preferring the ripe, moist meat
of melons—and Lorca's lover lying
in that crazy hard-on dream, oblivious
of what was going on, unconscious
of his own demise—with the poet gone
who would immortalize his soul?—and
the barrel of a rifle prodding Lorca's
chest like the insistent finger of Uncle
Sam, hard up against his anus, prying
open his mouth *muévelo, maricón* and
Lorca's face green as the craters
of his vellum moon, his body twisted,
a hibiscus against the dawn, stumbles
ahhh! as they jab him on, blindfold
filth across his eyes, *those eyes*, bind
laces from his shoes into his wrists so
when he staggers to the wall his shoes
drag through the gravel, unravelling
the earth's tears, the earth's dark song

> *drrrggge drrrggge dirige Domine*
> *Deus meus in conspectu tuo viam meam*

Lorca, my poet, shot down in prayer
while his lover unaware sleeps and dreams
of almond eyes and bougainvillea.
Homosexuals die violent deaths, Segovia
says, playing a Bach fugue on his guitar.

Nuyorican Lament

San Juan you're not for me.
My cadence quails and stumbles
on your ancient stones:

there is an inner beat here
to be reckoned with—
a *seis chorreao*, a *plena*,
an imbred *¡Oyeeee!*
and *¡mira tú!* against which
my Manhattan (sorry
wrong island) responses fall flat.

¡Vaya! How can I deal with that?

And yet ... once, long ago,
your beach was mine; Luquillo
was my bridle path to ride—
back then, before the turning of the tide
when Teddy's blue-eyed shills
secured the hill
and tried in vain to blot
the language out. But *patria*

is a sneaky word—it lies,
seeming to turn its back
upon itself—it lies,
through paling generations—lies
        and lies in wait:
the sleeping dog of nations
no translation can obliterate

(and when it's roused—
beware the bully
beware the apple pie).

I rode with purpose then,
back then, when
you were mine, harnessing
the strength of iron

in my thighs—
my eyes blazing with self, my self
        with pride—

and once, at La Parguera,
I was baptized
on a moonless night in spring,
emerging purged and
reinvented, the phosphorescent
spangles clinging
to my skin, signaling
the night to bless my innocence—

then, only yesterday—or so it seems—
I spent my youth
in La Princesa's dungeon
for unproved crimes
against an unloved nation—yes

only yesterday, I knew where I belonged,
I knew my part.

And now, you see me here,
a trespasser in my own past,
tracing a faint ancestral theme
far back, beyond the hard rock
rhythm of the strand.
I walk down El Condado, past
Pizza Huts, Big Macs and
Coca-Cola stands
listening for a song—

a wisp of song—

that begs deep in my heart.

Orphans

When my father died, leaving me
distraught for never having known
him as father, as friend,
for never having known myself

as child of one whose eyes and mouth
and temperament were mine, my mother
cautioned me, told me not to mourn
what I perceived as loss: you and I

are daughters of the wind, she said,
you and I are fathers of our souls,
sprouting intact like seedlings
from two wind-borne acorns.

We thrive on luck, she said,
there is no father's love in that.

At My Father's Funeral

My father, a free-thinker, who
insisted I be reared like him,
lies in his open casket,
the blood of Jesus dripping
on his clean white shirt,
El Grito de Lares pinned
to one lapel, *La Bandera*
to the other, and instead of
boleros or plenas permeating
the heavy incense of the chapel
a rosario of *Padre Nuestros*
and *Ave Marías* churns the air.

I study his hands, try to stroke away
the spots that will bury themselves
into my skin like spiders, brown
recluses, that will never let go.
Be careful, his doctor warns me,
your father died of skin cancer—
but at 93, I'd say he's entitled to go
as he pleases, and this ceremony
that accompanies his departure is
not my doing. I have no rights here.

My half sister removes the pins
from my father's lapels and presses
them into my hand like an omen.
You're the firstborn, she says.
We decided you should have them.
I pin them on my blouse.

At the cemetery, a handsome woman with
white hair stands on the sidelines
flanked by men in grey suits.
Lolita Lebrón, my sister whispers—

and it is 1954. I am in Holland
studying literature and art
when the news comes over the wires
and students at school start

asking me whether I'm ashamed of being
Puerto Rican and I in turn ask them
whether they feel shame for Hiroshima
or Dresden or Dachau—because *I* do—
and they can't understand that
it *all* has to do with me, with them—

and here's Lolita Lebrón, patriot
or terrorist, take your pick—
though she never fired a shot
(*I didn't come to kill, I came to die!*
she proclaimed, ready to give
her life for *el gran ideal*),
her sole aim to publicize the plight
of her besieged island. They stormed
the Spectator's Gallery—she and
three men—waving German Lugers
and their outlawed flag and
shouting *Freedom for Puerto Rico!*—
when one of the men went berserk
and began shooting into the crowded
floor of the House—congressmen
diving for cover, under desks,
behind chairs, five hit, bleeding,
visitors screaming for help.

It was a suicide mission: born
in Lares, she felt it was her destiny—
but how could she have known
the sacrifice would be her children—
her son murdered during the trial,
her daughter killed in an accident,
or so they said, and she in and
out of solitary confinement
for thirty-five years, unable to eat
or sleep, unable to breathe,
her hair turning white overnight,
like her heart, a dead weight.

The roster at the grave site reads
like a who's who of better days.
The leaders old and infirm come

on crutches and canes—but they come.
My other sister tapes their tributes.
They recite my father's poems,
sing songs I didn't know he wrote.
When they sing *La Borinqueña,*
the one song I do know, my words
are all wrong—this is a new version,
Lolita's version—and my anthem,
my sweet anthem, is no longer
a *danza*, but a marching song.

Your father was a great man,
they all tell me, *a great man.*

I look cautiously around me
and spot them—one, two, maybe three
dark-suited men in the distance,
blending into the trees, documenting
our sorrow with hidden cameras
and tape recorders. No one
pays attention to them—the F.B.I.
is as much a part of their lives
as the shadows their bodies cast
across my father's grave. I want to cry
out that I am innocent, that I
have nothing to do with violence—
I'm there because we share a name,
a face—but when I look at my sisters

I see my *fate*. The next morning
my half brother waits at the airport.
He sees Papi's slogans like
stigmata bleeding on my lapels.
Ten cuidado, he warns me, *they might
not let you out.* We embrace
and I see our shadows on the sidewalk
merge—when I kiss him it is as if
I were kissing myself goodbye.

Annunciations

On the eve of Desert Storm, December 1991

Robbed of Titian at the National Gallery,
where a line of tourists has already penetrated
the great hall like an undulating serpent
we opt for Mary and her jeweled herald,
Van Eyck's masterpiece, in whose presence
a poet we know almost fainted the day
before, and we, too, following that holy ray
from heaven's window to womb, words
cast upward toward the eyes of God like prayers,
feel compelled to bow our heads, to genuflect,
our very beings transformed into something humble,
full of grace—*Ecce ancilla Domine.*

I had spent the day defining language,
upholding the rights of artists
to create freely and without fear, and here
in the flesh, so to speak, the very essence
of creation having nothing to do
with laws, with rights, with regulations—*it is.*
Alone, it has the power to make us *tremble.*

Under a full moon, haloed and hallowed
in a Van Gogh sky, doming the spire and belfry
of the unfinished National Cathedral, we want
to fall to our knees, swoon, give thanks for what is,
for what this day we have been given. Nearby,

the Vietnam Memorial rises in a slow
wave from the depth of sorrow to overwhelm us
with its wordless accusations. Votives
like *luminarios* cast formal shadows
across the chiselled marble slabs, giving
voice to souls dishonored, flesh disowned.

Who are all these people bearing my name?

Your hand tightens in mine, a fist we share

and in a former life would have shaken
with our fathers at—*what*? What *then*?
What *now*? We follow the long, long wall
of dread, death pinned to our hearts
in yellowed ribbons, as we retrace
the steps of our own past, uttering
the same confession as the last time
we encountered shame, and the time before that,
and the time that is about to come—

forgive me, forgive me—I am not without sin

Field Day

The red-tailed hawk on the meadow by
my house is having a field day.
This morning he fell out of the sky
like a kite caught in a down wind,
clamped his talons into a skittering
squirrel and in an unbroken arc
landed on the largest limb
of a walnut tree across the green.
I watched the kill, enthralled by
the hawk's smoothness, precision, its
tenacity, reminded of the aerialist's
grand sweep as hanging upside down
from the trapeze he thrusts
his hands out just in time to catch
the tumbler by her wrists;
or even the swift curve of a stranger's
arm, swinging back and forth
like a pendulum as he passes you
on the street and snatches
your wallet, your identity, your worth.
Here, too, the squirrel never knew
what hit him, what gust
of hunger swept him off his feet.
Through binoculars I saw the hawk
with one quick jerk of beak and claw
defrock its prey, strip it of shape and
name, rob it of substance.
Sometimes in the early evening a vixen
will trot by, her kits by her side.
I grieve for them. Too heavy for
the hawk, perhaps, but oh those tails,
flaming and full and flagrant, bursting
behind them like flares,
can snare the senses, stir a woman's
envy, a man's unswerving thirst.

Commonwealth, Common Poverty

> *... a name means continuity with the*
> *past and people without a past are*
> *people without a name.*
>
> —Milan Kundera

A visitor comes from Hungary as from outer space
dropping into my Midwestern world with poems
about himself and that bracketed place he hails from.
And though the gift he brings is veiled, submerged
in allegory and myth, I recognize myself. Say
to him: this poem you read is about me. He smirks.

He has read his poems before and not been heard.
He is weary, somewhat cavalier. His body is taut like
a gymnast's. His eyes form flat black mirrors of distrust
adjusting to what he perceives as enemy turf. It's August.
He sheds his jacket, rolls his sleeves above his biceps.
A pulse in his temple keeps rhythm with his words.

He tries again, leads me as he reads. I see us both,
two generations earlier, perhaps three, running down once
familiar streets with new strange names, and I am plagued
by what I might have been had nothing changed,
had Teddy's boys not made it to the top of San Juan
Hill. Like him I, too, yearn for connections

between my parents' world and this one, long for
a tie, cut short by strangers—does it matter
that his were Russian, mine American; or that
his lines allude to Greeks and gifts of death, while
mine—because our history has yet to be revamped—
still lament the Massacre of Ponce? Here we sit

in a Kansas City motel, hearing what we say
translated by a man we have to trust—could be
a friend, could be a secret agent—a clean-cut man
in a banker's suit who keeps his jacket on,
claims he walked from Budapest to freedom, and

converts our pain into passionless sounds. Yes,

here we sit, feeling as our ancestors surely felt
the day their world shifted in its global socket
and everything they cherished perished in the quake,
leaving them disfranchised, disconnected from
their past, from each other, from themselves. How
they must have searched then for a look, a gesture,

a familiar word to ease their terror: the arch of a brow,
a jawline—*something* to bind them to their captors,
something so slight it might have gone unnoticed
had all remained whole. And we, their progeny, now
sit here immersed in Russian and American symbols:
we, their future, have become what they most feared.

for Zoltán Sumonyi

Psychomachia

Lucila Rieckehoff-Medina 1880–1967

Old woman, you took so long in dying,
proclaiming every year to be your last,
sighting death, describing its approach
through liver, spleen, and heart.

Old woman, you took so long in dying
they forgot you were alive. Not I.
I watched your body wither slowly, secretly,
your bones cringing from the lies they
forced into your veins. I saw your brain,
frantic in that halflight of infirmity,
spawn demons whose scorching tongues
and taunting wings fanned your despair.

I would come to cut your hair, your nails,
bathe your brittle shoulders with Bay Rum,
stilling the stale scent of death
with sweet perfume: fleeting memories
of palms and seas and youth and

you let go. Ever so slowly you let go,
easing an arthritic grip on sanity,
your devils fullgrown, lascivious, obscene;
and I? *¡Hipócrita!* you screamed,
because I said I could not see them.
How could I rid you of your incubus
or hear the vanquished demons rage and cry
confusi sumus!—if I could not see them?

I mourn you old woman, though I love you more
in memory than in fact: you had become
a stranger to me—distant, brooding.
I had to learn to look beyond your mood,
my mind screening out the present,
as yours the past. Perhaps we were meant
to meet on that unlabeled plain: I
to cradle you, you to teach me pain.

New York City Mira Mira Blues

From the freeway you can almost
hear them screaming in their
red brick coops (no hyphen, please)
        HELP ME, HELP ME
through glass grids silhouetted
like chicken wire against the
skyscrapers of Madison, Fifth,
Park, and lately Third Avenue,
where the old el used to shield
the homeless, now homes the shielded.
¡Ay, bendito! What did they do
to this city in their urgent need
to sprinkle liberalism like holy water
on the heads of the oppressors?
They should have played fair, *hombre*:
they should have left the *jíbaros*
in the mountains of their Isla Bonita,
perched like birds of paradise
on Cerro Maravilla observing
the rise and fall of the earth's curve
as it slumbers beneath the sea;
left them in El Fanguito, squatting
on the squatters squatting on the land
that once was theirs; left them
in Borinquen, where there was no cool
assessment of who owned what,
no color line splitting families
in two or three, where everyone,
todo el mundo, was tinted
with *la mancha de plátano*—but no,
they needed votes. Sure votes.
Had to buy them, fly them in by
planeloads, skies darkening thickly
with visions of *barrios* to come.
Since it was so easy getting in,
you'd think it would be easy getting out,
but where to go, and who'll take you in?
Take you in, yes; but give you shelter?

The Triborough Bridge, 50 years old
in gold cloth 50 feet high spanning
its towers, waves greetings to us as
we cross the East River, where I swam
as a child, running home as fast as
I could to stash my sopping clothes
in the hamper before Abuelita found
out and exiled me to my island bed.
Now dressed in punk colors, FDR Drive
shouts SAVE EARTH: GIVE A SHIT and
raises a SHAKER-KLASS-AMERICA fist
to the inmates on Welfare Island
whose view ah the view of the
newyorkcityskyline is optimum,
while the Old Rich on tree-lined
Sutton Place only get to see slums.
Welfare Island whose one aesthetic
function is to spew enough smoke
and soot into the air to obscure
Queens and itself, if the wind
is right, in a merciful eclipse.
Welfare Island, where our poet
Julia de Burgos was confined, forgotten,
all her protest silenced with yet
another 2 cc's of thorazine.

On 110th Street, my concrete manger
overlooking Central Park, only Spanish
signs remain to remind us of the second-
to-the-last immigration wave: Cubanos
seeking refuge when class status takes
a backseat to red slogans, red tape.
The Bay of Pigs non-invasion spurs
them on to invade us, Miami first, then
slowly up the coast like a spreading
thrombosis that ruptures in Nueva York,
where all Hispanics blend into one
faceless thug, one nameless spic.

The cab cuts like a switchblade
across the park; I try to hear Ives'

marching bands meeting in noisy combat
on Sheeps Meadow, but later sounds
intrude, reintroduce themselves
like forgotten kin—midnight, a baby
carriage, my mother crossing the park
from her sitter's on the eastside
to her husband's on the west. And she,
loving the leaves' black dance against
the night, recalls her mother's warning
that she not try to blot out the sky
with one hand, but oh! there beneath
the trees, the immensity of space is
palpable—she feels safe. And, lacing
the earth, a fragrance she cannot discern
causes her to yearn for home. She hums

half expecting the *coquís* to sing along.
It is that time of night when muggers
are out—even then before the word
was out—blending into shadows, bushes,
trees, like preview footage of Vietnam,
waiting to assault whatever moves,
whatever breathes. She breathes hard
but moves so fast they cannot keep up—
Westside Story before they learned
that death set to music could make
a killing at the boxoffice. With one
Robbins-like leap up a steep incline,
we escape; I sleep through it. Now
I'm wide awake watching every leaf quake
in the wind as her young limbs in flight
must have then, fifty years ago
on that moonless night in Central Park
where fifty years before that
sheep grazed and innocence prevailed.

We exit on 86th Street, head down
Central Park West, past the Dakota
to our safe harbor in the heart
of Culture and Good Manners with
Lincoln Center only steps away.
Next door a flop house. Old people
with swollen legs sunning themselves
on folding chairs, used shopping
bags with someone's trash,
their treasure, at their feet.
The buzzards of the human race
cleaning up other people's droppings.
We walk around them, as though
proximity could contaminate. Nearby
those less prosperous prop themselves
up against their own destruction.
I see my children stepping carefully
between them, handing out coins
like Henry Ford. I see them losing
faith, losing hope, losing ground.

But I am home, *home*, I tell myself.
Home from the wheat and the corn
of Middle America, where whole-
someness grows so tall you cannot
see the poverty around you, grows
so dense the hunger cannot touch you.
Home to the familiar, the past; my
high school moved comfortably closer,
renamed LaGuardia for the Little Flower
who captured our hearts with
Pow! Wham! and *Shazam!* on newsless
Sunday mornings during the war.
Home to my Westside condo with free
delivery from columns A to Z,
a xenophobic's dream come true.
Home to the city's long shadows
casting tiers up, across, and down
skyless streets and buildings,
an Escher paradox turning a simple
journey to the corner into a fantasy

65

in chiaroscuro. Yes, I'm home,
home, where my grandmother's aura
settles softly and white like
a shroud of down, stilling, if only
for a moment, the island's screams.

III. Singing the Land

Soy el río
la mariposa y culebra
—Julia de Burgos

An unsung land is a dead land, and
if we forget how to sing the land, the
spirit dies.
—Australian Aborigine belief

Is Eden out of time and out of space?
—W. B. Yeats

An Other Island

Oh, listen, for a moment! Listen
to the wheels of a cart grinding
crookedly up a dirt road in old San Juan.
Listen! Through the jalousie
windows you can hear the guttural
cry of the egg man—

¡Huevos! ¡Huevos frescos!
¡Huevos de esta mañana!

as he goes from house to house
dispensing freshly laid eggs like
early morning blessings. We stir
beneath our canopy of mosquito netting,
stir, in the soft flannel breeze
of summer in Borinquen, gauze
shimmering over us like a bridal veil.

But here, now, only a horse-drawn
carriage brimming with boisterous
students on spring break,
and I, bare and barely stirring,
in this New York City taxi heading west.

Out of Bounds in Kansas

for Pearse Mitchell

These days I live in a treehouse
above the green,
where golfers swing their arms and bodies
in time to the wind, in keeping
with the driven branches of the basswoods.

It is Labor Day. Hot September gusts
split the air like golf balls whizzing
down the treelined alley to the 16th hole.
I watch the hackers,
their white caps and gloves reflecting
the early morning light as they file by
in a rhythmless conga line,
lifting first one leg, then the other—
but no kick to it, no passion,
only the ritual motion of body like ball
dribbling from fairway to fairway.

Not my stepfather. He had a knack
for it. His feet in their metal-laden
multicolored oxfords trotted like a lithe fox
across the grass. "My heart quickens
when I see a green," he told us
that one time he came to visit.
And he might have stayed—his heart intact—
viewing the course each day
from our high perch, had not the ocean
beckoned to him—as it does me—to come home.

Santa Fe Journey

for Susan and Tom McGreevy

1. Monte de las Piedras Rosas

There's a piñon tree outside
    my window, full
of tiny silent verdins blending
into its sparse needles. I
    wouldn't have noticed them
but one bird fluttered,
    as if suddenly chilled,
its russet feathers like
    an early sunset signaling
a change in season; then
    the whole tree shuddered
and, a breath later, it is bare.

2. Los Alamos

Why the name? Not a poplar in sight.
Not a sapling, not a songbird. Not a soul.
In the circular distance
Las Truchas, implacable peaks (second
highest in New Mexico)
secure the sky to the land;
the pueblo bearing their name
reclining in the hollow of one slope—
waiting, watchful
of the encroaching barrenness below.

Crosses carved from the raw earth
lase lurid warnings across our path,
reminding us, *yes, this is the place.*

We drive past an old adobe hut. The face
of Christ, painted in a blaze
of reds and black across its whole façade,
looks back at us in pain and disbelief.

Los Alamos, Los Alamos,
sacred, secret origin of death—

> *the name explodes within my head,*
> *dustblood settles on my eyelids, my tongue.*

We slow down, as though searching for something,
something to still the shame.
A sign of hope, of purpose. Of forgiveness.

Silence. A dry silence. A dusty silence.

And in the shadow of the trading post,
half-hidden from the brutal sky,
sullen youngsters damn us with their eyes.

They do not wave as we drive by.

3. Promesas

To El Santuario de Chimayó,
as to the Ganges, they flock—
the needy, curious, doubting, and devout,
looking for a spiritual handout
from this "most holy national shrine"
(so named under the provisions, mind you,
of the Historic Sites Act of 1935).
They're coming "to witness, to commemorate
the history of the United States."
United States?—this here's MEXICO, hombre.

And I, the tourist, come too;
to pay homage, to honor—what?
A lost heritage? A dying legacy?
These strangers who speak my tongue
are not *my* people? I'm from Borinquen—
that tiny island drowning in a sea of Coca-Cola.
These people have their *patria.*

An old woman *jesusiando* follows
my pilgrimage into the dank, dark belly
of the sanctuary, her face parched
like the land she is condemned to till,
her fingers flitting from relic
to relic—touching, stroking,
needing to lay hands on her history, to feel

the pulse of her ancestral heart.
The walls are taut with hope and trust;
trinkets everywhere—charms, lockets,
wedding rings with tiny messages,
service medals, bracelets, dogtags—all
fabricating a haunting collage of life, death.
Of endurance. Ah yes, endurance.

A cabinet displays photographs of loved ones
with names like the five sons in that old song:
Pedro, Pablo, Chucho, Jacinto y José; and
letters signed *tu hijo, tu hijita,*

tu marido que te quiere siempre.
Siempre—what a warped and wicked word!

In the center of the room
plastic icons adorned with rosary beads
remind me of deer heads
during the Zuni Shalako—
    turquoise and silver squash blossoms
    wrapped around their slender necks
    to ward off the evil eye of winter—
and in the corners, totemic,
canes and crutches and discarded casts.

And, finally, *promesas*. Tacked to the walls.
Hand written promises to God:

> *This cross is a symbol in thanking you*
> *for the safe return of my son Juan*
> *from combat duty in Vietnam.*
> *I made a promise to walk 150 miles*
> *from Grants, New Mexico, to Chimayó.*

But what if Juan had not come back—what then?
Would his father have dissolved the covenant,
his rage propelling him to curse his God?
Or would he have submitted—
walking farther, seeking deliverance?

It's what my grandfather would have done.
I remember now, I am six, sickly.

My grandfather on his knees beside my bed.
I remember the promised curls
cascading down his chest
and over his vest like a tabard. Once
in a dream, I felt them soft against my cheek
and woke up weeping.

"Kitsch!" quips a man behind me.

The light outside is blinding.

4. Chimayó

A dog ambles across the empty dusty road
lifting his hind leg to pee on the garbage cans
of El Chimayó Café where

BURRITOS * TACOS
HAMBURGERS
Y
GAS

are sold. Round brown faces framed by crudely
lettered signs—a pink OPEN above,
COCA-COLA in chartreuse below—peer out at us
from the concession stand as we drive up.
On the adobe a painted hotdog trickles
crusty catsup and relish. We stop. Wait for gas.
Suddenly a car pulls up behind
imprisoning us in the past. A woman cautions
            ¡Mira—tengan cuidado!
Pointing to our captor, she motions
little circles around her temples and mouths
            loco, loco,
            esperen hasta que se vaya.

Dogs in slow motion—salivating, panting
like weary wolves—stop traffic as they sprawl
themselves across the road and lick their genitals.

Down here,
a brilliant heat subdues the evening,
while in the mountains, always the rain
falling in smudged streaks

like mammoth shades to earth

and always God hiding
behind every dwarfed juniper bush, chamiza,
ready to spring on smug Anglo skepticism
with some special sleight of hand—now
a simple dandelion, now a raspberry finch, all
ingeniously framed by a motionless sky
the blue of my youngest child's eyes.

And far in the background a Rothko mural
of muted mountains surrounds us
with peaks of brooding greens, grays, lavenders
lapping and overlapping. And always *there*
the hills, and always *here* the center, my center,
extending outward past the past,
far beyond the future—
for I was here before, even before
I drank the magic Chimayó potion
that obliterates time and space and boundaries,
restoring peace, oneness.

> *I am the bear that comes at nightfall*
> *to greet the new moon*
> *soy india, soy mexicana*
> *soy mujer*
> *soy*

5. Return to the City of Holy Faith

Signs back to Santa Fe are incongruous,
out of sync with this timeless world

> *Shirley's Pizza Parlor*
> *Nambé Bronze Works*
> *ICE*

What do I know of bronze and ice?
I'm of another age.

I want to tuck myself into a fold
of a withered speckled mossgreen mountain
and write my Latino soul's secrets
for my children

77

who may otherwise never know *me*.

Lightning like an arrow to an enemy heart
points the way home.
¡Mierda! It's raining in Santa Fe.
(My holy faith is being tested again.)
I still have to pack and catch the 7:15 flight home.
Home? I *am* home.

A final look.

The natives of Santa Fe know their place—
low earth homes blending with the clay ground.
They know the servants of the Lord
do not compete. They support the heavens
as do my hands when into evening
I reach up and cup the trembling stars.

We drive by a graveyard of unknown
New Mexican soldiers, their bravery
squeezed parenthetically between two insults—
BONANZA CITY on the left, USED CARS
on the right. Where in hell am I?
St. Francis Drive, the answer. *To the hills!*

Away! Away! *A las montañas,*
                    like Carlos, my fugitive uncle,
                    the Puerto Rican banner
                    tucked resolutely beneath his arm—
                    defying windmills, imperialism, death. *Away!*

Faith

for Philippe

Sometimes when I witness the blindness of faith
I feel cheated,
Robbed of a liturgical heritage that should have been mine.
But I've been exiled to a prosebyterian plane—insensate,
Incenseless, devoid of hocus pocus
With water no holier than Perrier.
I've had to endure tedium without *Te Deum*,
Listen to scriptures
In a raptureless take-it-or-leave-it vernacular. I left it,
Protesting its blandness, rejecting not faith
But the leveling down of faith to a line so fine it ceases
To divide the inner from the outer life—as though
The noises of the street
And the turmoil of the soul were interchangeable.

I have a friend, a good Catholic, who gets off on ritual,
Ritual for its own sake,
Much like good theatre, where you're so transported
By the trompe l'oeil sets, paste jewels, electric sunlight,
It doesn't matter whether the words fade
Before they reach your second-to-the-last-row seat—
The magic stays—night after night.
So, too, the magic of Hail Marys on the rosary or
The Latin Mass every Sunday of your life,
Fish on Friday, Benediction on Thursday—a predictable,
Dependable, inspiring show (makes you want to sing
And dance up the aisle, beating
Your breast and snapping your fingers to *Mea culpa*).

Oh, it should have been mine!

But I grew up in other people's homes, learned early
To distrust the permanence of words
And stones and flesh, not to mention
The father, the son, or the holiest of ghosts.
I *know* the curtain falls on all things. Still,

Sometimes, something deep within me hums
In a minor key,
Mouths syllables I don't fully understand or even hear and
When I least expect it, stuns me
With a right hook to the eye of reason.

Graffito

This morning I had my first flying dream:
not like my daughter who levitates,
then swims through space,

her Australian crawl cutting the clouds
with Olympic precision; not like my mother,
who springs like a high diver,

arms at her side, turning an occasional
back flip or half-gainer in mid-air
before landing on her feet.

No, in my dream I was a bird of peace,
scribing love against an overcast sky,
my cursive flight a caveat

from above—and all because a dinner guest
last night described his first kill,
his first feast of dove.

Glimpses of Light

1.

A brown towhee nudges us awake with its song.
Windows everywhere—sunlight
serrates our bodies, serves them up
on plum sheets we took for brown
in last night's dimness.
Past the picture window
I see myself both horse and rider caught
in the Sandía's lavender haunches, a white
cloud shrouding my body. Here,
in this bed, plums and purples and leftover dreams.

(I could settle for less.)

I must have lived out there once
on that transparent peak,
washed ashore by an inland tidal wave
that erupted in Utah, burst forth
from the entrails of the earth
in an insatiable longing for light.

Was I clay, then? I am still.

They tell me all elements in my body
come from earth and sea and sky.
Am I kin to tortoise?
Fired from phoenix ash? The Lost
Pleiad? Or *Hen to pan*—ouroboros?

The world beyond the window is impatient—
beckons us to hurry up, join our hosts
in their daily ritual labor to sculpt
the land around them. I dawdle.
Still lazy from sleep. Feel
drafts from an open door glaze
my skin with the scent of piñon.

2.

I am in an adobe womb about to be born:
the bed, my womb's placenta,
the sheets, purple and twisted, my umbilicus.
Thick posts support the walls
of my comfort, keep me from suffocating.

In this cell within cell I *know* the tree
is sacred, wood divine.
Poets, I beseech you—respect the tree.
Worship its bark, pray at its roots:
it yields words.

3.

Light makes fools of us.
I emerge from a darkroom of brushes and colors,
a room where I am temptress, queen,
only to catch a glimpse of myself
in a shiny car fender
as clown.

4.

At night I am in my rights. Days,
I play Colette, dress up in white, draw
the curtains against the light
till we turn young again in the mauve
kindness of each other's eyes—but then

I am condemned to recreate
the cursive shadows of the sun, coaxing thought
across the bleached pulp of day.

5.

Yesterday afternoon the mountains
bore charred streaks along their slopes;
low clouds cast shadows like reins
slowing my lope across the horizon.

Time to take stock, put it all together—
sandhya on Sandía—*ya es día.*

6.

From this room I can see the world
receding with the sun.
Evening shadows shape our bodies,
carve them and fatten them
like a ceramist adding a pinch
of age and then removing it
with forgiveness. Lying

beside you by this open window, stars
glazing our bodies with a hint
of caring, I feel blessed, somehow—
as though from this point on
I could go forward or backward in
time or space and it wouldn't matter,

as though for the first time I knew
that this silence enclosing me
in its cocoon will soon be shattered
by the heart's first song and
my life, long a solar eclipse,
is destined for the good side of the moon.

HE 2-104:
A True Planetary Nebula in the Making

On the universal clock, Sagan tells us,
we are only moments old. And this
new crab-like discovery in Centaurus,
though older by far, is but
an adolescent going through a vital
if brief stage in the evolution
of interacting stars. I see it
starting its sidereal trek
through midlife, glowingly complex—
"a pulsating red giant" with a "small
hot companion" in tow—and think
of you and me that night in August
speeding across Texas in your red
Mustang convertible, enveloped in dust
and fumes, aiming for a motel bed,
settling instead for the backseat of the car,
arms and legs flailing in all directions,
but mostly toward heaven—and now
this cool red dude winking at me
through the centuries as if to say
I know, I know, sidling in closer
to his sidekick, shedding his garments,
shaking off dust, encircling
her small girth with a high-density
lasso of himself, high-velocity
sparks shooting from her ringed
body like crazy legs and arms until
at last, he's got his hot companion
in a classic hold and slowly,
in ecstasy, they take wing and
blaze as one across the Southern skies—
no longer crab but butterfly.

Learning My Name

We have a dialogue, this tree and I,
back to my first lonely run across
the morning, light pursuing me
like a bandit threatening anonymity.
I point it out, now, to my husband,
Look! There it is—my tree.
But on that dawn, jogging up the hill,
my heart feuding with itself,
blood goosestepping in my temples,
my chest, I thought I'd die,
before I'd reach the top—still,
up I went, up the slick slope
to the plateau, where I collapsed
at the foot of the giant pin oak
and lay there in the green lull till
breath came easy, lay there
a good hour inhaling the dark fumes
of mould and peat moss and
regenerating worms. When I sat up
and looked around me, I was landlocked,
beached. I, who'd grown up defying
the surge and undertow of seas
and oceans—earthbound! Yet
I had come to cherish this land,
its contours comforting as dawn,
reassuring as my grandmother's arms
had been, ready always to bear my pain.
In the distance I could see a fox
strutting across the meadow, above me
sparrows weaving their nest, above
them a hawk on the lookout for game—
Oh, I was happy—I guess.
I leaned back against the tree,
patted the jagged bark behind me
in a reverse embrace and heard—
I swear!—clear as a whisper of love—
I heard my name.

GLOSSARY

Abuelita little grandmother.

A las montañas to the mountains.

Ay bendito (Dios) Oh blessed (God); typical Puerto Rican expression, said of anything that elicits pity.

Boriquén Taíno name for Puerto Rico.

Confianzuda a person who takes liberties, invades your space without your permission.

Confusi sumus (Latin) we are vanquished.

Coquí tree frog indigenous only to Puerto Rico; it cannot survive elsewhere.

Culipandeando swaying their hips (coined by Puerto Rican poet Luis Palés Matos to describe the walk of Haitian women).

Danza a slow Puerto Rican dance and its tune.

Dirige, Domine Deus ... meam (Latin) Direct, O Lord my God, my way in thy sight.

Ecce ancilla Domine (Latin) Behold the hand maiden of the Lord.

El Fanguito San Juan squatters' slums.

El gran ideal the great ideal.

El Grito de Lares The Cry of Lares, symbol of the Puerto Rican people's ongoing struggle for independence, their rebel yell. It is based on the colonists' failed attempt to gain independence from Spain by establishing the Republic of Puerto Rico in Lares, on September 23, 1868.

Esperen hasta que se vaya wait till he leaves.

Flamboyán a ubiquitous red flamboyant flower, its petals carpet the country roads of Puerto Rico.

Fuego fire.

Guanín gold medallion worn by the chief of the Taínos.

Hen to pan the One, the All, often inscribed on the ouroboros.

Hipócrita hypocrite.

Huevos frescos ... de esta mañana this morning's eggs.

Isla Bonita pretty island (nickname for Isla Nena Vieques Puerto Rico).

Jesusiando praying and crossing oneself.

Jíbaro hill-billy, peasant, now a national symbol.

La Bandera the Puerto Rican flag.

La Borinqueña the Puerto Rican national anthem.

Lares see: El Grito de Lares.

Malcriada spoiled child.

Mancha de plátano stain from the viscous secretions of the plaintain; refers to the "true" Puerto Rican or jíbaro, stained from peeling and eating plaintains.

Maricón derogatory term for homosexual.

Massacre of Ponce the police opened fire on unarmed nationalists (including women and children) as they marched on Palm Sunday, March 21, 1937; 100 were wounded, 19 killed.

Mastica tu comida, niña chew your food, child.

Microbios germs.

Mi querida hermanita my dear little sister.

Mira, mira tú look; also used as an exclamation to call attention; "hey!"

Muévelo move it.

Music notation beginning of the popular song "Puerto Rico."

Nuyorican Puerto Rican born in New York City.

Ouroboros serpent biting its own tail: symbol of the continuity of time, of life.

¡Oye! listen!.

Patria homeland.

Plena Puerto Rican folk dance.

Psychomachia the struggle for the departing soul by the good and evil spirits.

Sandhya Hindu meditation ritual.

Sandía mountain range visible from Santa Fe.

Seis chorreao Puerto Rican folk dance.

Siempre always.

Sobitos massages.

Soy india ... soy I am Indian, I am Mexican, I am woman, I am.

Taínos native inhabitants of Boriquén, an agrarian peaceful tribe of potters and weavers; those who were not decimated by the Spanish colonists committed suicide en masse.

Teddy's blue-eyed shills Teddy Roosevelt's Rough Riders who waged the campaign against the Spanish in the Caribbean during the Spanish American War in 1898.

Tengan cuidado be careful.

Te voy a dar una paliza, muchacha I'm going to whip you, girl.

Tu hijo ... marido your loving son, daughter, husband.

Uno ... cinco one, two, three, four, five.

¡Vaya! Go on!.

Ya es día the day has come